CARING FOR THE PLANET
SEAS AND OCEANS

Neil Champion

FRANKLIN WATTS
LONDON · SYDNEY

An Appleseed Editions book

First published in 2006 by Franklin Watts
338 Euston Road, London NW1 3BH

Franklin Watts Australia
Hachette Children's Books
Level 17/207 Kent St, Sydney, NSW 2000

© 2006 Appleseed Editions

Created by Appleseed Editions Ltd, Well House
Friars Hill, Guestling, East Sussex TN35 4ET

Design and production by Helen James

ISBN-10: 0 7496 5997 1
ISBN-13: 978 0 7496 5997 4

Dewey Classification: 333.91′ 6416

A CIP catalogue for this book is available from the British Library.

Photographs by Photographs by Alamy (ACE STOCK LIMITED, Brandon Cole
Marine Photography, Bryan & Cherry Alexander Photography, LOETSCHER
CHLAUS, Shaun Cunningham, David Noton Photography, Michael Dwyer,
Daniel L. Geiger / SNAP, David Hosking, ImageState, Kees Metselaar, Mira,
David L. Moore, Mark A. Johnson, Photo Resource Hawaii, PHOTOTAKE Inc.,
Pep Roig, Jeff Rotman, Andrew Seale, Slick Shoots, Stephen Frink Collection,
Steve Bloom Images, M I (Spike) Walker, WorldFoto)

Contents

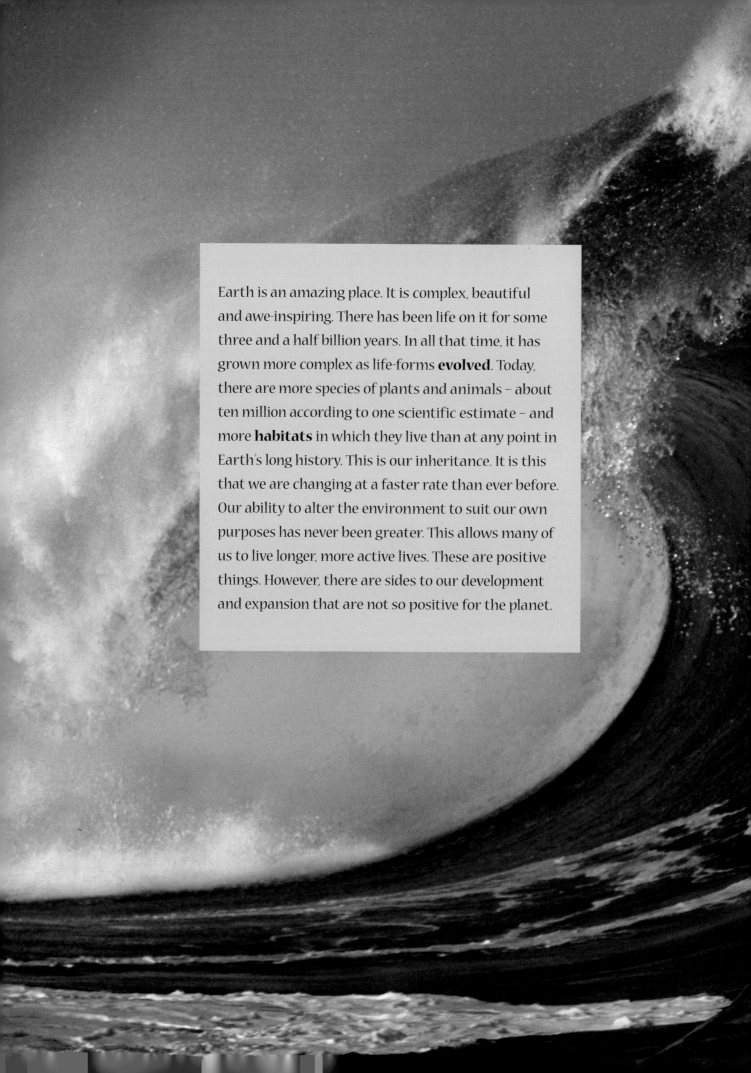

Earth is an amazing place. It is complex, beautiful and awe-inspiring. There has been life on it for some three and a half billion years. In all that time, it has grown more complex as life-forms **evolved**. Today, there are more species of plants and animals – about ten million according to one scientific estimate – and more **habitats** in which they live than at any point in Earth's long history. This is our inheritance. It is this that we are changing at a faster rate than ever before. Our ability to alter the environment to suit our own purposes has never been greater. This allows many of us to live longer, more active lives. These are positive things. However, there are sides to our development and expansion that are not so positive for the planet.

The ocean biome

Environmental scientists divide up the world into large natural zones called biomes. These biomes include oceans, deserts, **temperate** woodlands, rainforests, **tundra**, grasslands or prairies, and rivers and wetlands. Each biome has a certain type of climate and is characterized by its plant and animal life, which is adapted to live in the conditions it offers.

This book looks at life in the ocean biome and the threats oceans face today. It also looks at some solutions to these threats that may protect what is left of the natural world.

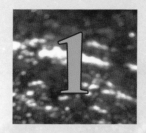

A blue planet

The oceans of the world are vast. They cover more than two-thirds of the surface of the planet and reach down to an average depth of 4,000 metres. They form the world's largest habitat and support tens of thousands of different species of plants and animals. They also help to support all life on land by providing much of the oxygen we breathe. The water cycle starts and ends with oceans and their salt water makes up 97 per cent of all water on our planet. Heat from the sun is distributed by the movement of water through ocean currents, affecting and regulating the climate all over the globe.

The health of the oceans is vital to our existence. They are the last and least affected environments on Earth in terms of human interference. In spite of this, they have never been as threatened by people as they are today. For decades, they have been used as dumping grounds for much of our waste, including nuclear material. Sewage, oil spills, chemical waste from industry, the litter of tourism around the popular beach resorts of the world – all show that we take the oceans for granted and have not looked after them with adequate care. Steam **trawlers** were first introduced in the 1870s, and we have been taking fish from the sea on an industrial scale ever since. In some parts of the oceans, certain fish populations are down 90 per cent, which has affected the **ecological** balance.

Scientists around the world have been monitoring the plants and animals of the oceans for many years and their research reveals how robust nature can be. For example, on a marine nature reserve in New Zealand, where fishing has been banned for many years, fish now teem in massive numbers. The relationships between all life-forms are delicate. Unfortunately, human communities have the ability to severely disrupt those delicate relationships.

Blue planet

A photograph of Earth from space, looking down upon the great expanse of blue water. The land mass of Australia is clearly visible at the bottom.

Pacific Ocean

A view out over the Pacific Ocean from the west coast of Oahu, one of the main Hawaiian islands.

A view from outer space

For human beings, land is extremely important. It is where we live our lives. We venture across the seas and oceans by boat and plane and occasionally swim at their edges for pleasure, but the kingdom of water remains an alien environment to us. Once in it, we are vulnerable. Underneath the water's surface, without special equipment, we can die within minutes. Yet all life started in the seas, and a view from outer space reveals that Earth is a blue planet. Land takes second place by comparison. Because of their vast size, the seas and oceans have been only partially explored and understood by scientists and environmentalists. However, we know that beneath their depths are the world's biggest mountains and deepest valleys. The largest creature ever to have lived, the blue whale, lives in the ocean. One of the greatest and most important annual events in nature takes place near its surface – the spring and summer bloom of **phytoplankton** in temperate seas. This complex and mysterious world helps sustain

all life on Earth and is one of the most important parts of our planet's life-support system. Take away the oceans, and our world would be lifeless and sterile.

Origins of life

All life began in the salty oceans millions of years ago. The oldest ocean was formed around 3.8 billion years ago. Single-celled bacteria, the first life-forms, appeared about 3.5 billion years ago. From the very beginning, the presence of oceans was intricately linked to emerging life on Earth. Today, there are probably thousands of species of animals and plants still undiscovered in the ocean depths.

Not all oceans – or even all regions of the ocean – support the same amount of life. One of the main factors in determining the density of life in the oceans is the amount of light that an ocean zone receives, with the top layer of the oceans getting

Great Barrier Reef
A marine scientist studies the Great Barrier Reef off the coast of Queensland in Australia. This enormous reef is one of the natural wonders of the world.

Minamata Bay

*In the 1950s, a tragedy struck in Japan that affected many people from a small fishing community. A factory accidentally leaked mercury into the sea. This pollutant found its way into the native fish and shellfish, which were eventually eaten by local people. Mercury collected and concentrated in their bodies, and they developed movement problems. Many had babies with defects, including paralysis, and some died. This event made clear to the world that the sea does not always disperse poisonous chemicals. Sometimes, toxins collect in seabed **sediment**, fish and seafood, becoming more concentrated and more deadly.*

the most light and therefore having the greatest variety and largest amount of life. Saltiness of the water is also important. The seas around the poles are far less salty than the Mediterranean, for example, and are home to abundant amounts of life, from huge whales to microscopic plants and animals. The temperature of the water is also a major factor influencing how productive an area of ocean can be. For example, cold water can hold more oxygen than warm water, which is often an advantage to animals and plants.

The human factor

An added factor in the modern world is an area of ocean's pollution level. Coastal waters and inland seas tend to have more pollution because of their closeness to human settlements and industry. However, recently tiny particles of plastic and other wastes have been found throughout the oceans of the world and on remote beaches and coastlines.

These must have been transported by waves and ocean currents over a period of time.

Pollution now extends to the seas around the North Pole and the huge continent of Antarctica. This means that no place on Earth is free from the effects of industrial waste. Certain types of pollution, such as mercury or chemicals such as **DDT**, can accumulate in the bodies of animals, including tiny zooplankton. Small fish eat great numbers of **zooplankton** and therefore collect large quantities of harmful chemicals in their bodies. Larger fish then eat great quantities of small fish and take in even higher amounts of chemicals. Finally, at the end of the food chain, there are humans. People eat the larger fish and run the risk of even greater concentrations of harmful chemicals in their bodies.

Oceans of the world

There are three main oceans: the Pacific, Atlantic and Indian Oceans. Scientists sometimes include the Arctic Ocean and the Southern Ocean, also known as the Antarctic Ocean. The Arctic Ocean is the smallest and is usually thought of as an extension of the Atlantic Ocean. The Southern Ocean is really a combination of the southernmost waters of the Pacific, Atlantic and Indian Oceans.

Seas are much smaller than oceans. Often connected by a narrow strip of water called a strait, seas can form a separate and distinct part of an ocean. For example, the Strait of Gibraltar separates the Atlantic Ocean from the Mediterranean Sea, and the Bering Strait comes between the Arctic Ocean and the Bering Sea. Some seas, such as the Black Sea, are totally enclosed by land. Sea water is salty like that of the oceans.

Oceans are very deep in places. The deepest ocean of all is the Pacific, which has a maximum depth of about 11,000 metres. The Arctic is the shallowest ocean, but still reaches depths of almost 5,500 metres, which is deep enough to swallow North America's Rocky Mountains. The temperature of surface ocean water varies from 29°C in the Persian Gulf to -2°C in Arctic waters.

Ocean sizes

Pacific Ocean: 179,700,000 square kilometres

Atlantic Ocean: 106,500,000 square kilometres

Indian Ocean: 75,000,000 square kilometres

Southern Ocean (Antarctic Ocean): 127,760,000 square kilometres

Arctic Ocean: 14,000,000 square kilometres

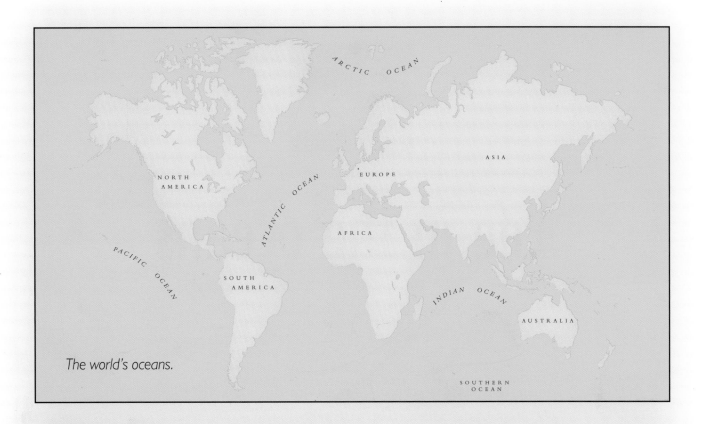

The world's oceans.

Pacific Ocean

The Pacific is the largest, deepest and oldest ocean in the world, although it is shrinking very slowly. It covers one-third of Earth's surface and at its deepest point reaches more than 11,000 metres at the Mariana Trench. Its average depth is about 4,190 metres, and it is probably around 200 million years old. There are more than 30,000 islands in the Pacific Ocean.

Atlantic Ocean

Half the size of the Pacific, the Atlantic Ocean is the second-largest ocean in the world. It is the saltiest of the major oceans and has the greatest **tidal range** – up to 15 metres in some areas.

The Indian Ocean

The third-largest ocean on Earth, the Indian Ocean reaches a depth of about 7,450 metres at the Java Trench. Around the Persian Gulf, the waters of the Indian Ocean are the warmest of any ocean.

Arctic Ocean

The Arctic Ocean surrounds the North Pole. It is the least salty ocean and is frozen over most of the year with ice that is between 0.6 and 4 metres thick.

Southern Ocean (Antarctic Ocean)

The Southern Ocean surrounds the South Pole and the continent of Antarctica, which has been called the last great wilderness on Earth. However, even here oil companies are pressing to explore the land and seabed for precious reserves of fossil fuels.

Life in the oceans

Life on Earth first started in the wide, salty waters of the oceans millions of years ago. Many species slowly adapted to life on land, but the oceans are still home to thousands upon thousands of different types of plants and animals. The variety is huge, and every conceivable **niche** in the ocean environment has been inhabited. This includes the immense coastal waters around the world, the depths of the oceans where very specialized animals live, the vast open ocean and the beautiful coral reefs. However, all these ocean environments are under threat from human interaction, with overfishing and pollution being the two main culprits. Life in the ocean is robust and adaptable, but it is not indestructible.

Webs and hains

As on land, the animals and plants of the seas need to feed and reproduce. The world's largest **ecosystem** provides all that is necessary for these processes to take place. All living things in the oceans are linked in a vast web of life. Food chains extend from phytoplankton and zooplankton to large sea mammals such as whales and the great predators of the seas, sharks.

One of the most common food chains is as follows: tiny plants (mainly **algae**, a type of phytoplankton) are eaten by tiny animals such as crab larvae, shrimps and krill. These, in turn,

are eaten by small fish. The small fish are eaten by large fish and finally, the larger fish are eaten by sharks.

A much shorter food chain bypasses some stages. For example, some giants of the ocean, such as basking sharks and whale sharks, eat tiny zooplankton. These massive animals swim through the water with their mouths constantly open, scooping up millions of microscopic creatures.

One of the major problems around the world occurs when one part of a chain is damaged. If small fish are harvested to near extinction by people, then animals further up the food chain may starve and stop reproducing. The smaller animals and plants normally eaten by the fish then grow in larger numbers, upsetting the ecosystem's balance.

From the shallow, warm seas of the tropical coasts to the icy waters around the North and South Poles, plants and animals

Basking shark

A basking shark swims through the sea with its mouth wide open, scooping up plankton. The basking shark can grow over ten metres long and is the second largest fish in the world.

Ocean acrobat

The humpback whale is known as the acrobat of the oceans, leaping into the air (or breaching) as shown in this photograph.

The humpback whale

This mighty creature of the open waters feeds on herring off the coast of Alaska in the summer months. It has to eat plenty of these fish to put on an incredible three to four tonnes in weight, which it stores as thick blubber. It then swims almost 4,000 kilometres to the waters off Hawaii to breed. During the journey, it stops feeding. It will fast for up to five months before it returns to its feeding grounds off Alaska.

have adapted to the water's depths and temperatures. These range from the sunlit surface of the open seas to ocean beds far underwater where no light ever penetrates. Environmental

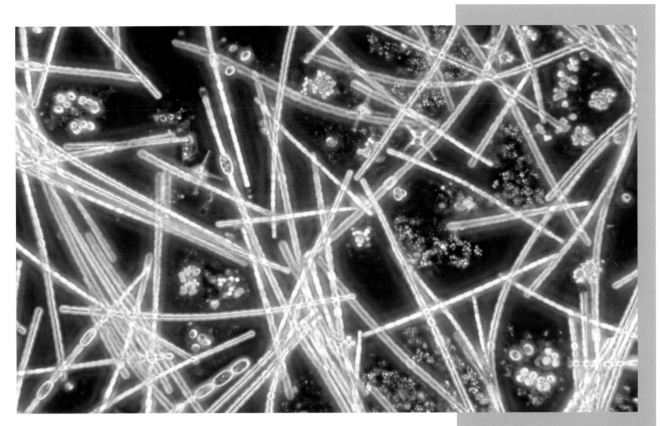

Amazing algae

Phytoplankton are green algae that multiply massively in a relatively short space of time during their spring and summer bloom. More than six billion tonnes of plant matter are produced in one growing season. These tiny creatures form the first link in the ocean food chain. Phytoplankton serve as more than a food source, however. These tiny sea plants use sunlight to produce nutrients for themselves in a process called **photosynthesis***. A by-product of photosynthesis is oxygen, used by all living animals in the sea and on land. More than half the world's oxygen is produced by phytoplankton, so any major imbalance in the oceans that might affect the reproduction of phytoplankton would have serious consequences for life on Earth.*

problems affect different zones in different ways. The deepest zones are almost untouched, while coastal zones have been severely affected by pollution.

Plankton

Phytoplankton magnified many times. These tiny organisms form the basis for the ocean food chain.

Cornish coast

The Atlantic Ocean meets the land on the Cornish coast. The constant pounding of waves has eroded the rock, causing landslides and the formation of small sea stacks.

Coastlines

The great oceans surround large landmasses called continents and thousands of islands. This creates millions of kilometres of coastline worldwide. Here, where land meets sea, is a special habitat that is constantly changing as the immense force of waves batters cliffs and beaches.

Intertidal zone

This is the thin strip of coastline that is submerged when the tide is in and exposed to the air when the tide is out. Organisms that live here, including seaweed and other algae, mussels, limpets, barnacles, crabs, shrimps, sponges and sea anemones, have evolved to cope with these constantly changing conditions. Many avoid being washed out to sea by attaching themselves to rocks. They live on whatever the tide washes up in the form of food scraps.

Continental shelf

This is the name given to the shallow area just beneath the waves that extends out from shorelines for an average of 75 kilometres.

Continental slope

The continental slope is a stretch of seabed beyond the continental shelf. This region slopes down to join the deep seabed, reaching a depth of about 2,500 metres.

Ocean bed

This region contains mountain ranges, deep trenches, volcanoes and extensive flat areas. No light ever reaches it, and the pressure of the water is so great that only a very few specialized creatures can survive here.

Vacuum cleaner of the ocean bed

*The humble sea sponge is an amazing creature. It can **filter** incredible amounts of water very quickly – around 5,000 litres every day. This volume of water is nothing, though, when compared to the amount filtered by the basking shark. This gentle giant, which can weigh five tonnes and grow to more than ten metres, feeds on plankton, which it sifts from the water. It processes about two Olympic-sized swimming pools worth of water every hour! Unfortunately, if the water these creatures are filtering is polluted, problems occur for the individual organism and for the entire food chain of which the organism is a part.*

Sea sponge

A tube sponge on the seabed off the Philippine coast in South-east Asia.

Amazing diving animals

Southern elephant seals have been recorded diving to the incredible depth of 1,700 metres when looking for food. Human divers, wearing special clothes called dry suits and breathing compressed air, may dive about 50–60 metres by comparison.

Whales are mammals, which means they breathe air, not water. However, they can dive to great depths and stay underwater without breathing for hours on end. When diving, they still need to communicate with each other. Being very intelligent animals, they have developed a complex system of calling to each other through the water. Their 'songs' sound eerie to humans, who still know very little about the habits of many kinds of whales.

Elephant seals

A pair of elephant seals on the island of South Georgia in the South Atlantic Ocean. These large animals can dive to great depths inn their search for food

Exploring the depths

*The first underwater vehicle was built in 1776 during the American
Revolution. However, it was not until the second half of the 20th
century that underwater crafts were used to study life in the
ocean depths. One of the most successful crafts was an American
submersible called Alvin. It was launched in 1964 and could
descend 4,000 metres below the surface. It made many dives and
brought back data to help scientists understand more about how
life works deep in the oceans. In 1960, a craft called the Trieste
travelled close to the deepest part of the ocean, more than
11,000 metres down. Even today, this remains the world's
deepest dive by a manned craft. Both manned and unmanned
crafts, known as remote-operated vehicles, or ROVs, are used in
exploration. However, there are still only a small handful of crafts
built to withstand the enormous weight of water that presses
down on everything at these great depths. This is one of
the reasons we know so little about the underwater world.*

Ocean explorers

*An artist's impression of
the submersible Alvin.
Deep submergence
vehicles (DSVs) can take
two hours to reach the
seabed, carrying a pilot
and scientists.*

Open ocean (pelagic waters)

The open ocean is the huge area of ocean far from land. It is divided into different depth zones. Most life occurs in the top zone, where light from the sun can penetrate the thin layer of water to provide a source of energy for plants and animals.

• Euphotic zone: the euphotic zone makes up the surface layer of water across the oceans. The key factor is that it allows light to penetrate. It can be as deep as 300 metres where the water is very clear, such as in the waters around Antarctica. Because light from the sun can easily penetrate this zone, plant life can flourish in the form of phytoplankton.

• Mesopelagic zone: this layer forms the region where limited light can reach. It stretches down from the euphotic zone to about 2,000 metres. This is the region where most sea creatures live, including sharks, whales, fish and giant squid. Some go to the surface to feed, and mammals such as whales go to the surface to take in air. There are about 20,000 different species of bony fish,

Sea spider

Sea spiders are highly adaptable animals found all over the world, from warm tropical seas to cold polar waters. They live in both shallow coastal waters and the deepest ocean beds.

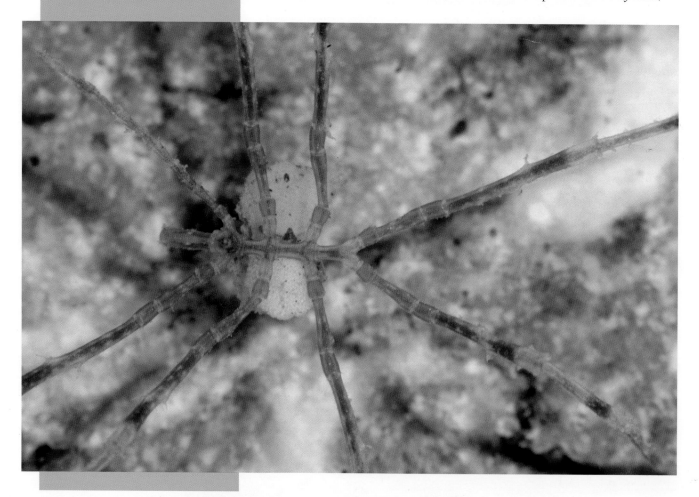

Black smokers

Colonies of life exist deep on the ocean bed, nourished by hot water thrown out of vents called black smokers. These vents reach down into magma under the ocean bed. The boiling water that comes out of them contains rich minerals that feed specially adapted bacteria. These, in turn, feed animals in the depths, such as tubeworms and giant clams. These colonies of life are unique in that their ultimate source of energy is not the sun, but hot, mineral-rich water coming from below Earth's crust. In recent years, scientists have been able to investigate these oases of very peculiar life-forms deep down on the ocean bed. They have discovered almost 200 new species living around black smokers.

and most live in this region, as do most of the 600 **cartilaginous** types of fish.

• Bathypelagic zone: this is the zone of total darkness in the oceans, which stretches down below 2,000 metres. It has been named Earth's inner space due to its darkness and utter mystery. Amazingly, many different types of animals and plants live at these depths, having adapted to the immense pressure and total lack of light in one of the most hostile environments on Earth. They live off each other and have developed special senses to track down prey or avoid being eaten. Because there is no light, the sense of sight is of little use. Instead, the animals feel vibrations. Creatures here have fabulous names and strange appearances – the ghost shark, hatchet fish, great swallower, oarfish, viperfish, rat tail and brittle star. Most feed on the dead bodies of animals that live higher up in the ocean zones. Once dead, animal bodies sink down to be consumed by these dark dwellers.

• Deep ocean beds (abyssal pelagic zone): on the floor of the oceans, where the pressure from the weight of water above is immense, life still manages to exist. For example, sea spiders up to 60 centimetres in size can live at depths of up to 5,000 metres, as can the tripod fish. There is no light, and these creatures are totally blind. They have learned to use other senses, such as smell and touch, to find their food.

Oceans under threat

There are now six billion human inhabitants on this planet, more than six times as many as there were just 250 years ago. Like all other habitats on Earth, the oceans have felt the strain of the human population's rapid increase and expansion. Today, humans catch more fish and seafood than ever before. We also extract more oil from the seabed, produce more waste and visit more coastal regions than ever before.

Abusing the oceans

People have exploited the sea for tens of thousands of years because it provides a rich source of food in the form of fish, crabs, squid, octopuses, mussels, lobsters and even seaweed. For most of history, the rate at which humans took food from the sea was easily matched by the rate at which natural reproduction took place to replenish these stocks. An easy balance was achieved. In the last 150 years, however, this balance has been upset. People have mechanized the way in which they fish and hunt at sea, using huge nets dragged by trawlers, expensive and accurate sonar and radar equipment for locating **shoals** of fish, and explosive harpoons for hunting whales. This has increased their catch dramatically, leading to a serious reduction in the number of such animals as whales, cod and herring. The Mediterranean Sea, the North Sea and the North Atlantic have all been overfished for generations, and we are now seeing the consequences. Cod, herring and haddock numbers are very low, and unless something drastic is done, they may not recover.

Dolphins, whales and seals have also been unintentionally trapped and killed due to the use of certain types of nets. Even the animals of the seabed are under siege from divers who collect shellfish and **crustacea** in nets. One extreme form of fishing uses dynamite to blow up reefs in tropical waters so that people can kill all the marine life and take the coral to be sold.

People also extract oil and gas from the seabed. They transport crude oil in huge tankers across the oceans from places of production to oil refineries. Accidents at sea result in oil spills, causing colossal damage to wildlife. Millions of seabirds have died, and entire areas of seafood have been wiped out. The coasts of Spain, France, Britain and Alaska have all been affected by spills.

Waste dumping

Dumping nuclear waste, hazardous chemicals and sewage from towns and cities at sea has been common practice for decades. Chemicals and waste from fish farms have also contributed

Fish traps

A fish trap rests on a coral reef in the Caribbean Sea. Fish trapping can badly damage these delicate reefs.

to pollution in some areas, such as Scottish sea lochs, in which salmon farms are located.

The oceans are enormous. Some scientists have estimated that they amount to around 1.3 billion cubic kilometres in volume. The sheer size of the oceans has led to the assumption that it is impossible for human beings ever to pollute them sufficiently to threaten their vital, life-sustaining role for land and marine life. However, animals such as beluga whales have been found to have high levels of poisonous waste in their bodies – waste that could only have come from dumping by humans.

Rivers

Pollution also washes into the seas and oceans through rivers, which collect agricultural waste, industrial chemicals and human domestic waste. All this eventually enters the sea and spreads out. The **estuaries** of many of the world's large rivers are often very polluted; the mouths of the Thames, the Rhine, the Rhone and the Danube in Europe have all suffered in the past from excessive pollution from industry and ships. However, massive clean-up efforts over the last decade have made dramatic improvements.

Comb jellies

When animal or plant species are taken from the place where they evolved over millions of years and put in another part of the world, severe ecological problems can occur. In a typical situation, prey and predators develop and evolve together to create a stable, well-balanced environment. As creatures low in the food chain reproduce, predators reduce their number to a manageable level. The amount of food, in turn, limits the population growth of the top predators.

In 1982, comb jellies were accidentally introduced into the Black Sea by a visiting ship from the United States. The result was a small ecological disaster. The comb jellies had no natural enemies in this new environment, so they bred unchecked. As the comb jelly population increased, they consumed more and more of the local fish and their eggs, as well as the plankton that fed them. Fish stocks in the Black Sea plummeted.

The Thames in London, for example, is cleaner today than it has been since the mid-19th century.

California kelp forests

There are about 10,000 types of seaweed worldwide, most growing in temperate waters. Kelp is one of the largest kinds of seaweed, reaching up to 60 metres in length. Great underwater forests of kelp grow off the California coast, which is washed by cold, nutrient-rich waters. Kelp forests are one of the wonders of the oceans. They have been likened to the giant redwood forests of California. Like the redwood forests, they are home to a huge variety of life, including fish, seals, sea lions, sea otters, whales, **molluscs** (such as abalone), and crustacea (such as crabs).

People have used kelp as an underwater crop since the early 20th century. It is a source of potash, a chemical used in gunpowder and the production of arms. It also contains a chemical called algin, which is used in food and cosmetics to help thicken or stabilize other ingredients.

Besides being affected by human harvesting, kelp forests are also affected by **El Niño**. When El Niño occurs, the growth rate of the kelp drops significantly. The temperature of the water in

Fast-growing forests

Sunlight filters through shallow waters on to a giant kelp forest. This type of seaweed can grow an incredible 30 centimetres per day.

Teeming reefs

A colourful grouper fish swims over a coral reef off the coast of Thailand.

the region rises, which is harmful to the plants. Sewage outflows also have a negative effect. Sewage in the water attracts large numbers of sea urchins to the area. They come because of the rich nutrients found in the sewage. But they also feed on the young kelp, which hinders the growth of the forests.

Coral reefs: a special habitat

Coral reefs are one of the natural wonders of our world. They are teeming, colourful, life-filled underwater gardens in shallow and warm waters in the tropics, close to the edges of continents and islands. They are made from tiny animals called polyps, which are related to jellyfish and sea anemones. Polyps live in harmony with tiny algae that supply them with nutrients. The polyp in turn gives the algae a home. When coral polyps die, they leave behind small, cup-shaped skeletons that form the well-known brittle reefs. Coral reefs grow at a very slow rate. The oldest remnants show that coral reefs existed 450 million years ago, and some living reefs are more than 10,000 years old.

Under threat: the Great Barrier Reef

Coral reefs are under threat around the world. People have taken parts of the reefs to sell to tourists. Pollution in shallow coastal waters has affected their growth. Coral has also been bleached by a rise in water temperature.

The Great Barrier Reef, the world's largest living structure, is about 2,300 kilometres long, reaching from the Gulf of Papua in the north to the tropic of Capricorn in the south. It is made up of around 2,500 separate reefs and encompasses more than 500 individual islands. It is the world's largest marine conservation area and is constantly monitored for problems. The massive reef is home to more than 400 different species of coral, 4,000 different types of molluscs and 1,500 different fish species.

In the 1960s, scientists noticed that the Great Barrier Reef had been infested with the crown-of-thorns starfish, which eats living coral. This was probably caused by people hunting the starfish's natural predators, the emperor bream fish and the giant triton mollusc. With fewer predators to keep them in check, the problematic starfish have multiplied out of control. The main loser in this disruption has been the habitat itself – the coral reef.

Great Barrier Reef

An aerial view of the Great Barrier Reef, the largest reef in the world, stretches down the east coast of Australia.

29

Bleaching

Coral reefs are very sensitive to temperature, needing water that is never cooler than about 20°C and never warmer than 29°C. Bleaching of coral reefs has occurred due to locally rising sea temperatures, thought to be caused by climate changes brought about by El Niño. These sensitive organisms die in water that is too warm – a rise of only one or two degrees is enough to start the bleaching process. The algae that live inside the polyp die, and the remaining polyp turns white and also dies. By the late 1990s, it was thought that more than half of the Great Barrier Reef had been affected by bleaching.

Dead coral

Dead, bleached coral in the waters around the Micronesian Islands in the Pacific Ocean. Bleaching occurs when water temperatures rise.

The North Sea

About 600 million tonnes of fish are caught every year around the world. Fishing communities today place so much pressure on the seas and oceans that regulations have been established in many places to help fish numbers. This includes the North Sea, which is one of the most productive stretches of water in the world, producing about 30 million tonnes of fish a year. The level of fishing taking place in the North Sea increased every year for decades up until the 1990s. Smaller and smaller cod and herring have been taken from the sea, and now the low population means that these species need protection.

Salmon fishing

As stocks of wild salmon have declined, some people have turned to farming this fish to supply our dinner tables. However, as with so many environmental problems, this is not as simple as it sounds. When salmon are intensively farmed – like chickens in pens on land – disease spreads quickly, with devastating results. **Antibiotics**, concentrated fish food and the chemicals needed to make a fish farm work build up in the waters around the fish farm. They collect in such high concentrations that they become a form of pollution in themselves. Some fish farms have become organic, which means that they do not use excessive amounts of chemicals and antibiotics. However, they produce fewer fish on average, and their produce is more expensive.

Farming fish

A salmon farm in Tasmania, Australia. Chemicals and antibiotics are used to control disease among the salmon, but these substances pollute the water.

Oceans and climate

Oceans affect all climates around the globe. Their influence on rainfall, air temperature and weather systems is enormous and complex. Oceans are also affected by the climate around them. As the world begins to feel the effects of a steady warming process, life within the oceans is disturbed. Most marine organisms are very sensitive to changes in water temperature. Their ability to reproduce can be affected, as can the ocean's complex food chains.

Ocean currents

Water in the oceans is moving all the time in a complex pattern of currents. Ocean currents flow around the world, moving warm water to cold climates and cold water toward the warm tropics. They are set in motion by many different factors, including the effect of different temperatures in the water, different levels of saltiness, Earth's rotation, winds blowing across the water's surface, even the shape of the seabed. There are two types of currents: surface currents and deep ocean currents.

Surface currents

Surface currents are moved by the action of wind on the surface of the oceans and by Earth's rotation. In the northern hemisphere, these currents move in a clockwise direction; in the southern hemisphere, they move anticlockwise. This is because of the

direction that Earth spins around its axis. Surface currents take warm water from the regions of the equator and the tropics to cooler regions. This helps some colder regions of the world stay a little warmer. For example, the western coastal regions of Scotland are washed by the **Gulf Stream**, which is a warm current that helps keep the temperature slightly higher than it would otherwise be. Palm trees and other exotic plants grow well in sheltered parts of Scotland's coastline, even though the country is far north. The western Arctic coast of Scandinavia is kept ice-free by the influence of warm-water currents as well.

Likewise, cold water from the north and south polar regions flows towards the equator. This makes coastal regions around southern Africa, New Zealand and parts of Australia cooler than they would otherwise be. The overall effect of these surface currents is to distribute heat from the sun more evenly across the planet.

Stormy seas

Storm waves pound the sea wall and send water across the road at a port in Massachusetts, USA. Scientists expect extreme weather to increase due to global warming.

Deep ocean currents

Currents are also at work on the ocean bed. Cold water sinks at both the North and South Poles and flows towards the tropics very slowly. As it does, it warms up and eventually resurfaces. It can take up to 1,000 years for this to happen. In this way, oceans act like huge radiators that circulate the sun's heat around the world, alternately heating colder lands and cooling warmer ones. This action is very important for the health of all life on our planet. This is because life has adapted to the huge influence this alternate heating and cooling has all around the globe. The scale it works on is truly enormous. If the influence were taken away, lands to the far north and south would freeze solid, and the tropics would become even hotter than they currently are.

Low islands

The low-lying islands of the Republic of Kiribati. These islands are vulnerable to the slightest increase in global sea levels, as they are only three metres high at their highest point.

The water cycle

*The action of the sun and presence of vast bodies of water drive the water cycle. Water in the seas and oceans is heated by the sun and **evaporates** into the atmosphere at a rate of about 950 cubic kilometres a day. It rises, and as it moves over land and is forced higher over hills and mountains, it cools and finally condenses, forming clouds. As clouds build up, rain falls on the land, watering plants and providing drinking water for animals. It drains into streams and rivers, flowing into lakes and eventually back to the seas and oceans. Then the cycle starts all over again.*

Global warming and ocean currents

*Some scientists think that **global warming** could slow down or even switch off the Gulf Stream and its extension, the North Atlantic Drift, the current that brings warm water to the western coasts of Europe. If this happens, parts of Europe could become colder as the rest of the world warms up. The scientists fear that as the Arctic and Greenland ice sheets melt, the addition of their fresh water to the salty waters of the region will change the way the Gulf Stream works. At the moment, dense, cold, salty water in the North Atlantic sinks to the bottom of the ocean and moves towards the equator, gradually warming up as it does so. Warm water from the Gulf moves north to replace this water, warming the region. However, if the water in the north is less dense and salty, it may not react in the same way, causing a weakening of the Gulf Stream. Scientists think that north-west Europe would become up to 9°C colder if this were to happen.*

Tsunami damage

A boat is beached in the middle of town on the island of Sumatra, carried there by the tsunami that devastated this part of the world on 26 December 2004.

Rough seas

A rough day at sea off the coast of British Columbia, Canada. The sea has an immense effect on weather and temperature along coastlines such as this.

The influence of the sea

Water holds on to heat longer than land does. This means that in winter, it cools more slowly than the land, helping to keep the temperature on the coast warmer than it would otherwise be. To get an idea of how much influence warm ocean currents have on coastlines, consider the city of Winnipeg in Canada. It is close to the centre of this immense country, and a long way from the nearest sea. Temperatures can reach 30°C during the summer and fall as low as -20°C in the middle of winter. The town of Victoria, on the other hand, although just as far north as Winnipeg, has a far less extreme climate. This is because it is on the coast in Newfoundland. In the summer, Victoria's temperatures reach 20°C, and in the winter, the average temperature is 2°C.

The ice caps

The North and South Poles are the coldest places on Earth because the sun, even during the short polar summers, shines at an angle on to the land. However, the great ice sheets and glaciers of the polar regions are retreating as the temperature of our planet slowly rises. The Arctic ice cap is today only half as thick as it was 30 years ago. About 24,000 square kilometres of the ice cap are melting each year. One of the effects of this massive ice melt is a rise in sea levels around the world.

El Niño

*El Niño is the name given to a warm current of water that appears off the coast of South America about every five to eight years. When it occurs, it disrupts the normal pattern of weather in the region and the habits of the area's wildlife, such as the anchovy shoals that provide an income for local fishermen. It affects the direction of the **trade winds** and causes severe hurricanes, floods, heat waves and droughts across the globe.*

El Niño typically occurs at the end of the year, around Christmas, and is marked by the appearance of warm water and the disappearance of the rich, cold waters that normally well up around the coast. It is worse some years than others. In very bad years, the fishing industry in the area collapses, birds stop breeding and local sea levels rise, causing severe flooding. The worst effects were recorded in 1982–83, when the Pacific islands of Hawaii and Tahiti were battered by huge storms, and Australia, India and southern Africa endured drought and famine. Scientists do not fully understand how this complex ocean current works, but the fact that it can have such devastating effects underlines how important it is to attempt to come to terms with it.

Storm victim

This marine iguana was a victim of a storm that hit the Galapagos Islands in 1998, thought to have been caused by El Niño.

The Larsen B ice shelf

In 1998, an area of ice measuring 150 square kilometres broke off of the Larsen B ice shelf in Antarctica. It was first noticed in satellite images of the area. Events such as this have led scientific research stations around the world to issue dire warnings about global warming.

'Our analysis of tree rings, ice cores and historical records from around the world indicate that the 1990s was the warmest decade of the millennium.... We are seeing changes in two decades that you don't expect to see in a lifetime. Nature is really confused.'
Tim Sparks, Institute of Terrestrial Ecology

The greater volume of ocean water from melting ice caps is not our only concern. Water expands as it gets warmer, so the increasing water levels will take up more space. This has led scientists to speculate on what might happen if this continues. Would low-lying islands and vulnerable coastlines disappear entirely if sea levels rose? During the 20th century, there was a 4°C average rise in sea temperatures around the world. Places such as Kiribati and Tuvalu, islands in the South Pacific which are less than four metres above the present sea level, coastal regions such as Bangladesh, and even coastal cities such as London, New York and Sydney, could be at risk in the future.

Melting ice

Ice melting in Patagonia, South America. This is a common seasonal event, but today it seems to be happening at an increased rate around the world as average temperatures rise.

The future of oceans

The oceans are huge, but they are not infinite. They have a massive capacity to cope with pollution, but they can be irreversibly damaged. Overfishing is the single most drastic action that humans carry out in the ocean ecosystem. But pollution through sewage, oil, chemicals and plastic waste now appears in every ocean on Earth. Climate change can have serious consequences for coral reefs and low-lying islands and coastlines around the world. It was once thought that toxins put into the sea would become diluted and disperse, but this is not always the case. In light of this, what has been done by scientists and politicians around the world to change these circumstances, and what can we as individuals do to help improve the future of our oceans?

International efforts

Through government and scientific research stations around the world, we are slowly learning more about how life in the oceans interacts and regulates itself, and thereby how to better conserve marine environments. For example, in the 1970s, the US Congress established national marine sanctuaries around the country. Today, there are 12 such sanctuaries, including those at the Florida Keys, the Hawaiian Islands, the Flower Garden Banks in the Gulf of Mexico, Stellwagen Bank off Massachusetts and the Channel Islands off southern California.

Hunted narwhal

The tusk or tooth of the narwhal, a whale found in the North Atlantic and Arctic Ocean. Today, only native Inuit of Greenland and Canada are allowed to hunt this animal.

International treaties have been passed to stop the worst acts of overexploitation. However, they are very difficult to enforce. Japanese and Norwegian people still hunt whales for scientific purposes. Traditional societies, such as the Inuit in Canada and Greenland, still get food by hunting beluga whales and narwhals, both endangered species. In 1997, the United Nations declared the International Year of the Coral Reef. The following year, they designated the International Year of the Ocean. These are attempts to get the nations of the world to work together in finding solutions to significant global problems.

An Alaskan mystery

In parts of western Alaska, certain types of marine life have been disappearing. The Steller's sea lion, the world's largest sea lion, lives in the region but is now facing extinction. Its population dropped by 80 per cent during the 20th century. The reason for this change has not been easy to unravel, but the answer so far reveals how complex and interrelated all life in the oceans is. The main clue in solving this mystery seems to be the humble herring. This fish is at the centre of many food chains. It is rich in calories and nutrients, and therefore a favourite source of food for many large predators, including the Steller's sea lion.

Recently, herring numbers have decreased for a number of reasons. Whales were hunted for many decades in the seas off Alaska until their

numbers dwindled to dangerously low levels. Humpbacks were reduced to 10 per cent of their original numbers. This decrease in the whale population led to an increase in the number of pollock, one of the whales' food sources. Pollock eat herring, so as pollock numbers increased, herring numbers decreased. There was also a total ban on pollock fishing called by Greenpeace, which might have affected the situation, enabling pollock numbers to increase –and herring numbers to decrease even further.

Herring numbers also decreased because of a decline in the number of shrimp – one of the herring's main foods – in the region. In addition, there has been a rise of a few degrees in sea temperatures in recent times. The rising sea temperature has had an effect on the cold, nutrient-rich waters that well up and feed herring. These rich waters have been pushed further east, leaving less for the herring to feed on. Oil spilled from the *Exxon Valdez* ship also adversely affected the herring population.

Threatened sea lions

A colony of Steller's sea lions on a rock in the Gulf of Alaska. With its population continuing to fall, this animal is threatened with eventual extinction.

As herring numbers decreased, the Steller's sea lion began to suffer. Although the sea lions also eat pollock, these fish have been called the junk food of the seas. They are not rich in energy-giving calories or nutrients.

The plight of the Steller's sea lion highlights just how delicate and complex food chains in the oceans are. Whaling was banned in the 1970s, and humpback whale numbers are now on the increase. This may help to restore the herring population, bringing the natural balance back in favour of the Steller's sea lion.

Stranded whales

A pod (or group) of pilot whales stranded on a beach at Cape Cod, Massachusetts, USA. Rescue workers are attempting to get them back out to sea.

Counting whales

Whales have been hunted in large numbers since the 19th century, and the numbers of many species were reduced to dangerously low levels. However, the 51 countries that formed the International Whaling Commission (IWC) put bans on hunting from the 1970s onwards to allow certain species, such as the humpback, to

increase their populations to around half their historic numbers. But establishing the numbers of humpback whales there were 200 years ago is no easy matter. This has traditionally been done by reference to ship logbooks, which put the historical number of humpback whales in the North Atlantic at around 20,000. Their number today in this region is around 10,000. However, scientists have recently done detailed DNA tests. These show that humpback numbers could have been as high as 240,000 in the North Atlantic. Now, the IWC has to decide whether or not to allow humpback hunting to start again, but based on the scientific evidence, humpback hunting should probably be postponed for decades to come.

Success for the sperm whale

Sperm whales have been hunted by people since in the mid-18th century. They were valuable because oil could be extracted from their bodies. It was used to make candles and was very clean when burned. Up to 5,000 whales a year were killed around the world by whaling fleets. The whales were probably saved from extinction because paraffin replaced whale oil. This meant that the hunting of sperm whales stopped almost entirely without an international ban. Other types of whales hunted for their meat have not been so fortunate.

Monitoring the seas

Making laws to help protect the seas and oceans around the world is one thing. Making sure that those laws are obeyed is another. Monitoring the condition of marine life and the quality of the water that supports it is therefore vital to the success of the movement to protect this biome. Monitoring also enables scientists to study the many forms of ocean life and their complex relationships through the food chains. This helps them predict where things are going wrong and gives them a chance to see if positive human intervention can help the situation.

Conservation organizations

There are more than 300 organizations around the world – as well as countless concerned individuals – monitoring the health of our oceans. The largest organization is the Great Barrier Reef Marine Park off the east coast of Australia, covering 35 million hectares. The largest in the US is the Channel Islands National Marine Sanctuary off the coast of southern California. Here are some other important organizations involved in looking after our seas and oceans.

• **Friends of the Earth**   www.foe.co.uk

Founded in 1971 in Britain, Friends of the Earth is now one of the world's best-known and most respected environmental pressure groups.

• **World Wide Fund for Nature (WWF)**   www.panda.org

Founded in 1961, this Swiss-based organization raises money to fund conservation operations around the world, focusing in particular on endangered animals.

• **Greenpeace**   www.greenpeace.org.uk

Founded in 1971 in Canada, Greenpeace has grown to become one of the world's biggest and most influential environmental pressure groups. It campaigns all over the world on behalf of the environment.

• **International Union for the Conservation of Nature (IUCN)**   www.iucn.org

This organization publishes *The Red Book*, which presents the most comprehensive picture we have today of the state of the planet in terms of threats to species.

What you can do to help

We can all help the great oceans of the world cope better with the growing population and demands of humans. Here are a few ways you can help.

• Think carefully when disposing of plastic wrappers and containers. Try to buy food products that aren't wrapped in unnecessary plastic.

• Recycle as many plastic, glass and metal products as you can.

• Conserve water by not wasting it – for example, by using a rain barrel to collect rainwater to use in the garden; turning off the tap while brushing your teeth; and putting a brick in the tank so that less water is used when flushing the toilet.

• All river waste and sewage eventually ends up in the sea. Be careful about waterways near you, and do your best not to pollute rivers, ponds or lakes.

• Use fossil fuels as sparingly as you can. This includes petrol and diesel in cars and electric and gas appliances around your house.

• Join a marine conservation group and get involved in finding out more about the fascinating world of the oceans.

Further reading

Ecosystems and Environment Anne Fullick and Chris Oxlade (Heinemann Library, 2000)

First Encyclopedia of Seas and Oceans Ben Denne (Usborne Publishing, 2001)

Seashore (Eyewitness Guides) Steve Parker (Dorling Kindersley, 1998)

What's Under the Sea? Sophie Tahta (Usborne Publishing, 2001)

The Seas Around Us Rachel L Carson and Ann H Zwinger (OUP, 1991)

Ocean Worlds Francesca Baines (Two-Can Publishing, 2001)

Websites

Oxfam
www.oxfam.org.uk/coolplanet/ontheline/explore/nature/oceans

Corals and Coral Reefs
http://www.seaworld.org/infobooks/Coral/home.html

Dive and Discover: Expeditions to the Seafloor
http://www.divediscover.whoi.edu

Nova Online: Into the Abyss
http://www.pbs.org/wgbh/nova/abyss

Oceans Alive!
http://www.mos.org/oceans

Ocean Planet
http://seawifs.gsfc.nasa.gov/ocean_planet.html

Glossary

Algae   A large and very diverse group of simple plants, ranging from single-celled organisms to enormous seaweeds. Algae are found both on land and in the oceans.

Antibiotics   Chemicals that help fight bacteria which cause diseases. Today, antibiotics are made in laboratories, although they also occur naturally in some plants.

Cartilaginous   A type of fish that has a skeleton made out of cartilage, instead of bone. These fish include sharks and rays.

Crustacea   The class of animals that is defined by a hard outer skeleton or shell. Examples include crabs, lobsters, prawns, barnacles and woodlice.

DDT   Abbreviation for dichloro-diphenyl-trichloroethane, a chemical used to kill pests, such as lice, that spread disease. It is banned in most countries today because it is highly toxic.

DNA   Abbreviation for deoxyribonucleic acid. DNA carries the special code that is passed on by parents to their offspring and that gives the instructions that make up the characteristics of each individual organism.

Ecological   Relating to the study of living organisms and their relationships with the environment.

Ecosystem   A natural unit of the environment in which all of the plants, animals and non-living components depend on each other in complex ways.

El Niño   An event that occurs around Christmas every five to eight years in the Pacific Ocean off South America, in which an irregular warm swell of ocean replaces the normally cold-water currents.

Estuaries   Places where rivers meet the sea, often called mouths of rivers. An estuary is the area that is influenced by the tides coming in from and retreating back out to the sea.

Evaporates   When water is heated and turned to vapour, it evaporates. Evaporation is part of the water cycle.

Evolved   Scientists believe that life on Earth has developed, or evolved, over billions of years. The theory of evolution claims that all life has come from single-celled forms and has slowly become more complex.

Filter   Some sea animals can take water into their bodies and remove, or filter, tiny plants and animals found floating in it. This is how they get their food.

Global warming   The process by which Earth's climate is thought to be getting warmer through an increase in greenhouse gases, including carbon dioxide and methane.

Gulf Stream   A warm ocean current that originates in the Gulf of Mexico and flows north past the east coast of North America, then heads east across the Atlantic around Newfoundland.

Habitats   Parts of an environment that are self-contained, supplying the needs of the organisms that live within them.

Molluscs   Animals that do not have backbones and have bodies divided into three parts – a head, a foot and a body. Mussels, oysters, snails, slugs, octopuses and squid are all molluscs.

Niche   The place within a habitat that each living organism occupies. This includes the way in which an animal or plant uses its habitat – what it eats, where it sleeps, and the environmental conditions it favours.

Photosynthesis   The process by which green plants on land and in the oceans turn sunlight and carbon dioxide from the atmosphere into oxygen and food for themselves.

Phytoplankton   A general name given to the many different types of microscopic plants that live in the oceans.

Sediment   Materials (such as small particles or rock and vegetation) that settle at the bottom of a river, lake or sea.

Shoals   Large numbers of fish of the same type swimming together.

Temperate   A term used to describe a climate that is neither too hot nor too cold. Temperate zones are halfway between the hot tropics and the cold poles.

Tidal range   The difference in the height of the sea between high tide and low tide.

Trade winds   A name used by seamen to describe the common, or prevailing, wind that blows toward the equator.

Trawlers   Fishing vessels that use a large net, which they drag along behind them to scoop up fish.

Tundra   Land close to or inside the Arctic Circle, where the layer of soil just below the surface is permanently frozen because temperatures are low all year round.

Zooplankton   A general name given to the many types of tiny animals that float in the oceans and seas, including krill.

Index